Acknowledgements

This guide was written by HSL with the assistance and support of the Agricultural Lime Association, the Confederation of Paper Industries, the Freight Transport Association, the Road Haulage Association, the Society of Motor Manufacturers and Traders, Institute of Transport Engineers, and Wincanton.

The author also gratefully acknowledges the information and advice provided by Tata UK Ltd, HSE, VOSA, Humberside Police, Suffolk Police, and the Metropolitan Police.

A Professional Driver's Guide to Safe Loading and Transport

Load safe, road safe
– a professional driver's guide to safe loading and transport

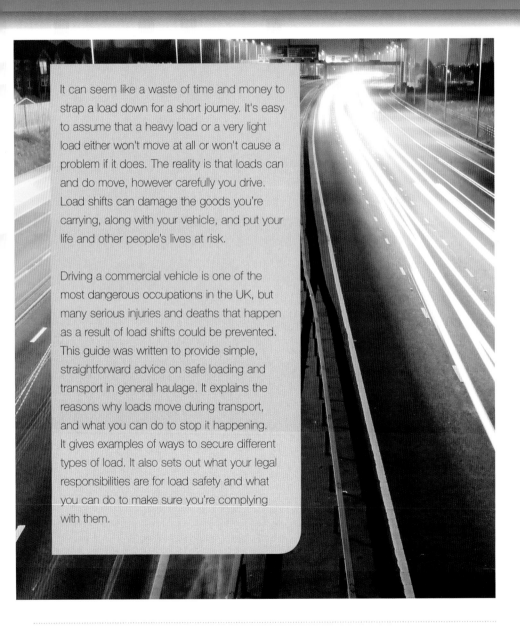

It can seem like a waste of time and money to strap a load down for a short journey. It's easy to assume that a heavy load or a very light load either won't move at all or won't cause a problem if it does. The reality is that loads can and do move, however carefully you drive. Load shifts can damage the goods you're carrying, along with your vehicle, and put your life and other people's lives at risk.

Driving a commercial vehicle is one of the most dangerous occupations in the UK, but many serious injuries and deaths that happen as a result of load shifts could be prevented. This guide was written to provide simple, straightforward advice on safe loading and transport in general haulage. It explains the reasons why loads move during transport, and what you can do to stop it happening. It gives examples of ways to secure different types of load. It also sets out what your legal responsibilities are for load safety and what you can do to make sure you're complying with them.

Contents

The basics of load shift

Wearing a seatbelt when driving is something most people do instinctively these days. Seatbelts work by securing the wearer to the vehicle, so they move when the vehicle does. If you don't have your seatbelt on, and the vehicle suddenly slows down, your body keeps moving forward at the same speed, so it feels like you're being thrown forward.

Anything you carry on or in a vehicle will behave in exactly the same way.

Because the load isn't part of the vehicle, it won't always move at the same time as the vehicle if it's not secured. Even heavy loads can, and do, move in normal driving conditions.

Load shifts often occur under braking. As the vehicle brakes, the load is still travelling at the original speed. If the load is not secured, it carries on moving forward at the same speed as the vehicle slows down. This means that the load will slide forward on the load bed.

The basics of load shift

The same thing happens in reverse when the vehicle accelerates. As the speed of the vehicle increases, the load is still moving at the original speed. This means that the load will slide backwards on the load bed.

Forward or backward movement of the load relative to the vehicle can be made worse if the vehicle is travelling up or down a slope as it accelerates or brakes.

If there's a large gap between the front of the load and the vehicle headboard or bulkhead, a load can move forward and hit the headboard. The headboard is the last line of defence for the driver – if the load smashes through the headboard, you are in serious danger. Drivers have been killed by loads that have come through the headboard and into the driver's cab.

Loads are also likely to shift when the vehicle is cornering. If the load is not secured to the vehicle, it won't necessarily turn into the corner when the vehicle does. This means it can slide sideways on the load bed. This effect can be increased if the road is cambered.

The basics of load shift

It's often assumed that heavy loads don't need to be secured because the weight of the load will hold it in place on the load bed. Unfortunately, this isn't correct: the forces exerted on the load while it's travelling are much higher than when the vehicle is stationary. Even heavy loads can move during transport. Uneven road surfaces, potholes, and speed bumps can all increase the risk of the load moving.

Once a load starts to move, it is potentially dangerous. It is much easier to stop a load moving in the first place than to try and 'catch' a load that is already sliding. Heavy loads have the potential to cause a lot of damage if they fall off the vehicle, while even light loads can cause accidents if other drivers swerve to avoid them.

Often shifted loads are contained by the vehicle body but that doesn't mean they are safe, particularly when you come to unload. Loads, or part loads, that are resting against the curtain of a curtain-sider or against the rear doors of enclosed vehicles and containers can fall out as soon as the curtain or doors is opened. Sloping or cambered delivery sites can increase the risk of unstable loads falling out of the vehicle. A lot of accidents during unloading happen as a result of poorly-secured loads falling off or out of delivery vehicles, and the driver is often the one who gets hurt. The injuries can be relatively minor, like bruises and sprains, or more serious injuries like concussion, dislocations and broken or amputated limbs. They can even be fatal. It's in your interest to make sure that the load is secured properly.

What the law says

Drivers and operators must comply with road traffic legislation and health & safety legislation. A load doesn't need to actually shift for an offence to be committed in either area of law – what matters is the risk of harm to either the driver or to other people.

Advice for drivers

You are legally responsible for your vehicle on the road under the Regulation 40A of the Road Traffic Act 1988 introduced by the Road Traffic Act 1991 and Regulation 100 of the Road Vehicles (Construction and Use) Regulations 1986. This means you must be sure of the safety and roadworthiness of your vehicle and the safety of the load you're transporting. If someone else has loaded the vehicle for you, you should be sure that the vehicle and its load are safe to go on the road.

A shifting load can kill. If the load comes through the vehicle headboard, the next impact will be with the back of your cab. A load shifting to one side on a round-about or a motorway slip road could cause a rollover. A load – or part of the load – falling from the

vehicle could hit another vehicle or a pedestrian or cyclist. You don't have to be driving too fast for a load to shift. Depending on the policy of the site where your vehicle is loaded, you may or may not be required to witness or be involved in the loading of the vehicle/trailer. If it is necessary for you to witness vehicle loading, this should be from a safe position, away from vehicle movements. You should, in any case, check the load when loading has been completed or get written confirmation from the consignor that the load is properly loaded and secured.

Section B

What the law says

Check that:

 The load is placed against the headboard if possible or, if there is a gap, that an intermediate bulkhead is fitted or blocking or dunnage is used to fill the gap to prevent the load sliding forward;

The load is loaded so its weight is distributed evenly across the vehicle If the load is stacked, or if you are driving a double-deck vehicle, the heaviest items should be at the bottom with the lighter items at the top;

The load is secured to prevent it sliding or toppling. The curtain of a curtain-sided vehicle is not normally strong enough to secure the load so unstable goods should be in a transport frame or similar;

The load has additional securing if the vehicle is to be transported by sea;

Load restraints such as bars, chains and straps are in good condition;

You know of any particular conditions at the delivery site/s you are travelling to, such as restricted access or a sloping site.

If you see, hear or feel the load move while you are driving, slow down (don't slam on the brakes!), and pull up in a safe place as soon as possible. Think about what you were doing when the load moved – if you were braking the load has probably shifted forward; if you were cornering it has probably shifted toward the side of the vehicle. It can be difficult to know how much a load has shifted inside a curtain-sider. Sometimes there will be an obvious bulge in one of the curtains, but this isn't always the case. The safest way to assess the load shift is via the rear doors.

Don't undo any lashings over a load unless you are sure it is stable. Drivers have been killed after unfastening lashings on unstable, shifted loads.

Get advice on what you should do next. Someone who has experience of dealing with shifted and/or unstable loads can help you or your employer to decide what the safest option is.

If your vehicle is stopped in a dangerous place (for example, on a motorway slip road exit), you or your employer may decide that you should move to a safer location at low speed so that the load can be assessed further. This should only be done if it would be more dangerous to stay where you are, and you and your employer should think very carefully before deciding to continue.

 You should not continue your journey if:

- you believe you are in danger in any way because of the movement of the load;

- the shifted load is significantly affecting the stability of the vehicle or your control of it;

- or you think there is a risk of any part of the load becoming detached or falling from the vehicle.

Remember that if any part of the load falls from the vehicle on the road, or you lose control of your vehicle because the load is shifting, other road users or pedestrians could be seriously injured or even killed, and you, the driver, could be held responsible and charged with dangerous driving or causing death by dangerous driving.

If you have any doubts about the safety and stability of your load, you should not continue your journey. Whatever pressures you're under to get the job done, remember that it's your licence, your livelihood, and your life that are at risk.

Drivers and operators should be able to show that the way the vehicle has been loaded does not endanger the driver or other road users. Drivers will have different levels of responsibility depending on whether they are employed by someone else or owner drivers.

Advice for Vehicle Operators

It is in your interest to ensure that loads carried on your vehicles don't shift – apart from your legal duties under road traffic and health & safety legislation, load shifts will damage your vehicles, the loads carried, and potentially your reputation as an operator. The driver is not the only person responsible for the safety of the load.

The Road Traffic Act says that anyone who causes or permits a vehicle to be loaded may be held responsible if the load is dangerous, and employers have duties under health & safety legislation to ensure the safety not just of their own employees but of anyone affected by their work activity. This includes sub-contract and agency drivers you may employ, anyone who loads and unloads your vehicles, and other road users.

Advice for Vehicle Operators

You should ensure that your vehicles are loaded so that they are safe for transport on the road and arrive in a safe condition for unloading. Your drivers should be aware of the basic principles of load shift and how to prevent it, and you should make sure they have the training and equipment they need if they are responsible for securing the load. Drivers should be made aware of how the vehicle is to be loaded even if they are not involved in loading; their experience and knowledge may help the loader/s identify any problems before the vehicle sets out on its journey.

Encourage drivers to report problems with loads so you can see whether there is an underlying issue. Don't automatically assume that poor driving is to blame for load shift; loads can and do shift under normal driving conditions and drivers won't report problems if they are unfairly blamed for them.

If you identify a recurring problem with loading or unloading, talk to the consignor or delivery site and try to resolve it.

Drivers carry heavy responsibilities when they are out on the road and can feel very alone when something goes wrong or if they are unhappy with how their vehicle has been loaded. You should support your driver if they refuse to take a load they think is dangerous onto the public road; it may be that the driver has not fully understood the loading method and the consignor can reassure you, or you may agree with the consignor that the load can be reloaded to the driver's satisfaction.

If a load shifts during the journey, you should help your driver decide whether it is safe to continue, getting advice from someone with experience of dealing with load shifts if necessary. Loads can shift even at very low speeds, so you should think very carefully about telling the driver to continue.

Remember that it could be your driver's life at stake if the load moves again. You have a legal responsibility to take reasonable steps to ensure his safety.

If he does continue to either the delivery site or another location, you should make sure they know the vehicle is arriving with a shifted load and are equipped to deal with it.

Carrying out a load risk assessment

A loading plan that travels with the load can help the driver show the enforcement authorities at the roadside that the vehicle has been loaded correctly.

Employers and the self-employed have a legal duty under health & safety legislation to assess the risk of what they do.

Risk assessment is not a difficult process: all you need to do is think about what you do, what could go wrong, and what you need to do to prevent anyone being injured if it does go wrong. You only need to record the assessment if you have 5 or more employees, but writing it down can help you identify the real risks in what you do.

It is a common misconception that risk assessment means removing all risk of danger. The key phrase is 'reasonably practicable'. This means that you have to take action to control the health and safety risks in your workplace except where the time and cost of doing so is grossly disproportionate to the reduction in the risk.

Example of how risk assessment can work in practice

A small company operates flatbed HGVs delivering goods to multiple delivery sites. Drivers are currently unloading the vehicles by climbing onto the load bed via the under-run bars to direct unloading by fork lift trucks operated by the delivery sites.

There are two main risks to what the drivers are doing: falling off the vehicle either while climbing onto the load bed or while standing on it, and being struck by a fork lift truck as they stand on the load bed.

Falling from height is one of the most common causes of injury in the transport industry – you don't have to fall far to be seriously hurt or even killed. The easiest way to control the risk in this case is to remove the hazard – is there a need for the driver to be standing on the load bed in the first place? Being struck by a fork lift truck is also a very common cause of injury, so it makes sense to keep the driver out of the immediate unloading area if you can.

It's better to do a short, practical risk assessment than a very lengthy, complicated risk assessment that no one ever reads! HSE produces a simple guide to risk assessment, *Five steps to risk assessment*, which can be downloaded from the HSE website,

www.hse.gov.uk

Warning
Fork lift trucks

Load safety:
getting the load from A to B

It's often assumed that the driver is the only person legally responsible for the load once the vehicle goes out onto the road. This is not necessarily the case.

In terms of responsibility there are three primary roles:

 Driver – the individual taking the vehicle onto the road

 Consignor – the company or individual responsible for placing the load onto or into the vehicle

 Operator – the company or individual responsible for transporting the load to its destination.

For some loads, one person will have all three roles. For most loads, however, there will be more than one person or company involved in loading and transport, and everyone has responsibility for making sure that these activities are carried out safely.

Where there is more than one person or company involved in loading the vehicle and transporting, it should be very clear who is responsible for what, particularly for multi-drop deliveries where the vehicle may be re-loaded or the load re-arranged by other companies. Communication can help to avoid many common unloading problems.

Load safety:
getting the load from A to B

1. The five principles of load safety

Securing a load for road transport may seem daunting at first, but the basic principles are very simple.

1. Choose the right vehicle – using the right vehicle for the load can make it much easier to secure the load.

2. Load the vehicle properly – the load should be loaded against the head board and with the centre of mass as low as possible. If the load is not loaded to the headboard, think about how the load can be prevented from moving forward. You may need additional lashings, or chocks or blocking.

3. Choose the right securing method – not all loads are the same and not all vehicles are the same. Webbing straps or chains are common ways to secure loads but they are not necessarily right for every load.

4. Use enough load restraint – accidents can occur when drivers and operators underestimate how much restraint is needed to keep a load on the vehicle. The forces acting as the vehicle travels on the road are much higher than the static forces.

5. Communication is the key – reporting near-misses and other issues such as restricted access to delivery sites or cambered delivery sites can prevent future accidents. Drivers should be given clear information about the loads they carry, how they are to be unloaded, and what they should do if the load shifts. A loading plan that travels with the load can be useful for everyone involved.

Load safety:
getting the load from A to B

What is the centre of mass?

The centre of mass is, basically, the tipping point of an object. On the average person, the centre of mass is located round about the level of the belly button. If you stand upright and lean forward while keeping your body straight, you find that you will start to topple over and you instinctively move your feet to keep your balance.

As you lean forward, your centre of mass also moves forward, so your weight is starting to topple you over. Moving your feet brings your centre of mass back into line so you keep your balance.

2. Choosing the right vehicle

The easiest way of securing a load is to use the body of the vehicle to prevent movement. If the load is loaded against the headboard, and the gaps between the load and the structure are minimal, the load is secured within the body, but only as long as the body structure is strong enough to withstand the forces acting on it.

If gaps have to be left – for example, the load has to be placed back from the headboard – then chocks, blocking or dunnage can be used to fill the gap between the load and the body structure.

Choosing the right vehicle for the loads to be carried can make securing the load much easier. Buying a highly specialised vehicle type for particular loads can be a good investment, but for most operators transporting a variety of loads this will not be feasible. With thought, loads can be secured on any vehicle.

Load safety:
getting the load from A to B

EN 12642 and the XL Standard

EN 12642 is a European Standard (BS EN 12642 in the UK) that sets out strength requirements for vehicle bodies. Vehicles constructed in the UK don't have to be constructed to EN 12642.

The Standard defines two types of vehicle body: an unreinforced body (L) and a stronger, reinforced body (XL). The curtains of an L curtain-sider can't be used to restrain the load but the curtains of an XL vehicle are allowed to restrain up to 40% of the vehicle payload, as long as certain conditions are met. The test certificate supplied with the vehicle will specify these conditions, but they might typically include:

 The load must fill the load bed from front to back, with a gap of no more than 80mm (approximately 3 inches) between either side of the load and the side walls;

 The load must be stable;

 The weight of the load must not exceed 40% of the rated payload of the vehicle. For a vehicle rated for 24 tonnes this means 24 pallets, each weighing no more than 400kg;

 The coefficient of friction between the load and the load bed must be greater than 0.3. For many load and vehicle combinations, friction matting between the load and load bed will be needed to meet this requirement.

Loads can be secured on L vehicles and unrated vehicles, and there is no requirement to use XL vehicles. However they can be useful for high-volume, low-density loads, and also as back-up containment for hazardous loads.

Section C

Load safety:
getting the load from A to B

Different bodywork types have different advantages and disadvantages.

Flatbed vehicles are easy to load and unload, and can be used to transport many different types of load. Curtain-siders have many of the same advantages as flatbeds, but the curtain helps to protect the load from the weather and keeps it out of sight. Box-sided vehicles have a rigid structure that can be used to contain the load, which can be particularly useful when you're transporting palletised or boxed loads that completely fill the load bed.

Vehicles should ideally have rated attachment points on the chassis if lashings are to be used to secure the load.

Attachment points in the load platform itself are a good alternative. Curtain-siders not constructed and tested to at least the EN 12642 XL standard are essentially flatbeds and should not be used without load restraint such as lashings.

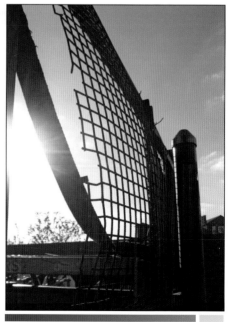

Load Safe **Road Safe**

Load safety:
getting the load from A to B

Lashings should be secured so that forces are transmitted into the vehicle chassis. Sheeting hooks welded or bolted to the load bed are not suitable attachment points.

The headboard of the vehicle is a critical part of the load securing system and for some loads, such as pipes or sheet steel, it may be necessary to specify a reinforced headboard. The purchase stage is also a good opportunity to work with the bodywork manufacturer to specify additional equipment, such as access equipment or fall arrest systems if you regularly have to access the load platform.

Anything attached to the superstructure of a non-reinforced body structure is not load restraint equipment. This includes webbing straps suspended from rails in the roof of a curtain-sider.

Load safety:
getting the load from A to B

3. Loading the vehicle

Loading the vehicle correctly is an important part of good load securing and time spent at the planning and loading stages can reduce the risk of delays and product damage due to load shift, as well as more serious consequences.

A loading plan can help to record the important information needed to secure a load properly and provide instructions to loaders and unloaders. This is particularly useful for multi-drop deliveries where the load may have to be re-arranged.

The higher the position of the centre of mass of the load is, the more likely it is that the vehicle will rollover. Loads should be arranged so that the heaviest items are as low as possible, with lighter items stacked on top if necessary. Where vehicles are loaded in drop order, it is important to consider the effect that has on stability, particularly on double-deck vehicles.

Some loads are more dangerous in terms of load safety than others. High-risk loads include:

- Metal pipes, sheet or bar
- Reinforced concrete
- Bricks, stone or concrete
- Vehicles (including scrap)
- Plant machinery
- Reels (steel, wire or paper)
- Kegs and barrels
- Stacked loaded skips
- Empty skips stacked more than 3 high
- Metal castings
- Glass
- Containers/work cabins

Load safety:
getting the load from A to B

For multi-drop loads, it may be necessary to re-arrange the load as it diminishes to make sure that the vehicle doesn't become top-heavy or that the weight of the load is offset. Lighter, crushable items should be protected from the weight or possible movement of heavier items. Where mixed loads are regularly carried, partition bulkheads within the body can help to separate fragile loads.

Ideally the load should be placed so that it is in contact with the headboard, but this may not be possible if doing so would overload the front axle.

If the front axle is overloaded by placing the load against the headboard, the load should be moved back and the gap between the load and the headboard packed, or the load chocked or blocked.

Likewise, the centre of mass of the load should be in front of the centre of the rear axle/s so as not to overload the rear axles, and to ensure that there is enough weight on the steer axles.

Load safety:
getting the load from A to B

For heavy loads, it is very important to distribute the weight of the load between the axles to minimise flexing of the chassis or bodywork.

Items with projections, or items with a small cross-sectional area such as pipes or bars, should be loaded to minimise the risk to the driver and others if load shift occurs.

Items should generally not be loaded at an angle over the headboard, as the headboard will act as a launcher under braking.If items are to be carried in this way, a dedicated restraint system should be used to ensure that the load cannot be launched from the vehicle.

Loads should be stable when any restraints are removed. Low, wide items are stable; tall, narrow items are often not.

Unstable items should be made stable – by placing them into a box or stillage, or by using a transport frame.

Unstable loads should not be secured by lashings alone - they can topple over as soon as the lashings are removed for unloading - so there is a benefit in making sure that the load is stable.

Make sure you think about how you can secure a diminishing load if you are making more than one delivery. A load that is secured safely when it leaves the despatch site may be insecure once a few drops have been made. You should also think about whether the load will need to be re-arranged to keep it in a safe condition or prevent axle overloading, and who will do this. You may need to use additional restraints once there are gaps in the load.

Load securing equipment

Securing a load effectively means thinking about the **load securing system.**

The system has to secure the load to resist forces equal to the entire weight of the load forward and half the weight of the load to the side and rear.

The system is made up of:

- The body structure of the vehicle;

- Chocks, blocking, cradles etc;

- Lashings or other restraints;

- The friction between the load and the load bed.

Making good use of the body structure and chocks, blocking or cradles means that fewer lashings will be needed to secure the load.

There are many ways of securing loads and it is important to make sure you are using the right equipment for the job. Using unsuitable equipment can slow down loading and unloading or even put you at unnecessary risk.

Some types of equipment are not suitable for securing loads. These include ropes used instead of rated lashings, buckle straps suspended from a roof rail, and the curtains of a standard curtain-sider.

Securing a load doesn't mean you have to use lashings, but they are an easy way to secure a load. There are different types of lashing and different ways of using them, so it's important to make sure you're using the right lashing in the right way.

Webbing lashing straps are used for many different types of loads. Straps are relatively inexpensive and simple to apply to the load.

Straps can be put over the load (friction lashing), wrapped around the load (belly-wrapping), or attached to lashing points on the load (direct lashing).

Friction lashing works by increasing the downward force on the load bed. The straps should be at as steep an angle as possible. Straps at a very shallow angle are not effective and another securing method should be used instead. The number of straps you need to secure the load may not be as simple as you think.

The British Standard BS EN 12195-1:2010 gives an equation that can be used to find the number of straps you need but strap manufacturers also provide simple tools to find the number of straps needed for a load.

Sometimes the number of straps suggested may seem excessive. This is normally due to:

 Not loading to the headboard – placing the load against the headboard or putting some thing in the gap between the headboard and the front of the load can significantly reduce the number of straps needed;

 The angle of the straps is too shallow. Try increasing the height of the load using light weight packing to increase the angle;

Load securing equipment

The friction between the load and the load bed is too low. Metal-on-metal loads will have a particularly low coefficient of friction. Try using friction matting between the load and the load bed to increase the friction.

If the number of straps required still seems high, it may be that straps are simply not the right securing method and you should consider a different method. When using straps with sharp or abrasive loads like metal or concrete, think about how the strap material can be protected using edge protectors or sleeves.

When securing crushable loads, or loads that are likely to settle, it can help to use boards along the outer edges of the load, or a pallet placed on top of the load, so that the force of the strap is distributed over the load.

Straps should never be knotted or passed around sharp angles, as this will reduce the strength of the strap. Don't use the excess from one lashing to form a return lashing.

Webbing lashings are very vulnerable to damage and should be checked at regular intervals.

Even age can significantly reduce the strength of a strap. A strap originally rated for 5 tonnes may fail at a load of less than a tonne after a few years of heavy use. The ageing process can be seen in the fading of the webbing material, and felt in the increasing brittleness of the webbing.

Chain lashing

Nets and tarpaulins

Chain lashings will often be used in the same way webbing lashings are used.

Chains are not as vulnerable to damage as webbing straps but they should still be checked at regular intervals.

Some loads require a combination of load restraint and containment, or the restraining force needs to be distributed to prevent the load being damaged. Nets and tarpaulins rated for load securing can be a good way of securing these loads.

Nets and tarpaulins used for load securing should be checked regularly to make sure there is no damage.

Load securing equipment

Bars

Positive fit

Bars are often used to secure rollcages in box-sided vehicles, though they may also be used with palletised loads.

If the load completely fills the load bed from the headboard to the rear doors, and the side body structure is strong enough to hold the load in place, you may be able to transport the load without any other securing. This is called positive fit. You can't use this method with a flatbed or standard curtain-sided vehicle, because of the lack of side containment. If you are using an XL-rated curtain-sided vehicle, the certificate that comes with the vehicle may show the conditions you have to fulfil in order to use positive fit.

Bars can be very effective at preventing load movement, but it is very important to make sure that the bars are a close fit to the load. Bars may not be effective in securing heavier loads and may become damaged. It is very important to check bars and the end fittings for damage at regular intervals.

Fahrzeugaufbau entspricht
Véhicule conform á la norm
Vehicle body in compliance with
Mustermann AG

EN 12642-XL

2006

Securing methods for different load types

1. Steel

Steel is a high-density, high-risk load and the consequences of load shift can be extremely serious. Movement of the load endangers:

 The driver, if the load slides forward during the journey or shifts sideways and causes the driver to lose control of his vehicle;

 Other road users and pedestrians, if the load shifts sideways or slides backwards and falls off the vehicle;

 Unloading personnel, if the load has become unstable during the journey and collapses during unloading.

It is very important to load steel loads so that they are stable on the vehicle without relying on lashings. This may mean using chocks or blocking to make sure the load is stable.

Even though steel is heavy, the weight of the load alone should not be relied on to hold it in place. The friction between individual items in the load, and between the load and the load bed, can be very low, particularly for painted or coated products and cold rolled products. If the vehicle is loaded in an uncovered area, wet or icy weather conditions can also reduce the positive effect of friction.

Steel should be loaded so that it is against the headboard of the vehicle, if possible. Loading to the headboard also means that the headboard can be considered part of the load securing system, and that means the number of lashings required will be much less than for a load loaded away from the headboard.

The headboard should be strong enough to prevent the load moving. If the load comes through the headboard it will go into the driver's cab – the headboard is critical in protecting the driver. For the same reason, the load shouldn't be loaded above the height of the headboard unless precautions have been taken to stop it sliding forward.

If it isn't possible to load to the headboard, or the headboard isn't strong enough to restrain the load, or the load is designed to be loaded away for the headboard, you need to make sure that the load is secured properly to stop it sliding forward uncontrollably.

This will usually mean you need to use more lashings on the load and you should think about using blocking, cross-over lashings, or an intermediate bulkhead at the front of the load to stop it sliding forward.

It is much easier to stop a load from starting to move than trying to catch it once it is moving!

Once the load is loaded it should be secured with lashings. It's very important to ensure that all parts of the load are secured. Building the load into a 'pyramid' shape can help to ensure that the lashings are in contact with the whole load and stop individual items sliding or toppling. Loop lashing ('belly-wrapping') is particularly useful in securing bundled products.

Securing methods for different load types

Chain lashings are very effective in restraining steel and are not damaged by sharp edges like webbing lashings. If webbing is used, it should be protected from any sharp edges by using webbing sleeves or edge protectors on the load.

Side posts or side boards help to protect both other road users and unloading personnel and are a useful way of ensuring the load doesn't endanger anyone if the lashing system fails for any reason.

Steel may be unloaded by fork lift truck or by crane. Try to avoid having anyone standing on the load bed during unloading, but if it cannot be avoided then you need to think carefully about where they should stand, communication with the fork lift truck driver or crane operator, and whether they need fall arrest equipment.

Securing methods for different load types

2. Bags and sacks

FIBCs, sacks and other bags may become unstable during transport and put the driver or anyone else unloading the vehicle at risk. It is important to make sure that the bags do not become unstable.

Where possible, load to the headboard. Bags can be secured using lashings, or by using tarpaulins rated for load securing.

Tarpaulin systems may be particularly useful if the bags are open or if the load is being transported on a flatbed and weather protection is needed.

When loads are stacked, the lower level needs to be strong and stable enough to support the upper level/s.

FIBCs, sacks and bags are usually not suitable for stacking, as the bags on the lower level do not provide a stable base for the upper level.

3. Coal bags

Coal bags should be secured for transport but it is important to also think about how the vehicle will be used. For domestic delivery, the driver will need repeated access to the vehicle at the roadside and some securing systems may put him at additional risk of falls or manual handling injuries. Operators should consider the overall risk when deciding how to secure the bags.

One of the easiest ways to secure coal bags for transport using flatbed vehicles is to use side boards to contain the load within the load bed.

Bags should be loaded against the headboard and they should not be stacked over the height of either the headboard or the sides of the vehicle. As long as the bags are contained within the structure, they do not present a danger. Bags transported as palletised loads should be treated as any other palletised load.

4. Palletised loads

Palletised loads are probably the most common load type in the UK. All kinds of loads are transported on pallets and it is important to think about what method of securing is suitable for the load being carried. Loads should be shrinkwrapped or otherwise secured to the pallet; shrinkwrap also helps to keep individual items together. It is important to make sure that the shrinkwrap goes around the pallet as well as the load – the aim is to make sure the load doesn't separate from the pallet.

For non-crushable loads, the easiest way to secure pallets is to use webbing lashings across each row of pallets.

This method works well on loads where the pallets are the same height. For multi-drop loads, loading in drop order, with the first delivery at the rear of the vehicle/trailer and the last delivery loaded against the headboard, ensures that the load is always loaded to the headboard.

Securing methods for different load types

A curtain-sided vehicle built to the EN 12642 XL standard may be able to transport pallet loads without lashings, as long as you make sure you comply with any restrictions shown on the test certificate. This will usually include minimising the gap between the sides of the load and the curtains, and increasing the friction between the load and the load bed using friction matting.

Lashings may not always be appropriate for delicate or crushable loads. There are several ways of securing crushable palletised loads.

A box-sided body can be used to transport pallets without lashings, as long as the load is loaded to the headboard and the gap between the load and each side of the vehicle is not more than 80mm (approximately 3 inches).

Remember, an XL-rated vehicle is normally rated to contain 40% of the rated payload. For example, with a rated payload of 24 tonnes, you could transport 24 pallets each weighing no more than 400kg.

A vehicle not explicitly built to the EN 12642 standard may be constructed in a way that makes it suitable to carry loads without restraint, but an operator must make sure that the structure is strong enough to at least match the XL requirements. This can be established through calculation or through testing.

Securing methods for different load types

Reels and coil are high-risk loads, as they can be very likely to move (roll) on the vehicle. It is very important that they are secured properly to prevent movement.

Reels and coils can be transported in different configurations.

The easiest way to transport heavy metal coil is on vehicles with dedicated coil wells, which provide a physical barrier to movement. Used in combination with lashings, this is a good securing system.

Paper product reels may be transported on end or on reel. When transported on end, the easiest way to transport reels is by using rigid-sided vehicles fitted with a walking floor to make loading and unloading straightforward and remove the need for warehouse personnel to enter the vehicle body.

As with other loads, the gaps between the load and the side walls should be as small as possible.

When transporting on reel, or when transporting on end in curtain-sided vehicles, physical restraint should ideally be provided by chocks or blocking used in combination with lashings.

Crushable reels can be protected by using edge protectors to distribute the force of the lashing.

6. Rollcages and roll containers

Rollcages are commonly used to move household goods and groceries, and are generally transported in rigid-sided single or double-deck vehicles.

Sideways movement is unlikely to be a problem with rollcages if they are loaded across the width of the vehicle, but it is important to ensure that they cannot roll forwards or backwards on the load bed.

Rollcages should be loaded to the headboard of the vehicle if possible. If there is a reason for not loading them to the headboard, an intermediate bulkhead can be constructed using restraint bars attached to the vehicle sides.

Restraints – either bars or webbing lashings – should be used every three rows of rollcages to prevent the load from rolling backwards.

It is particularly important to ensure that the back rows are secured to minimise the risk of cages falling out when the rear doors are opened.

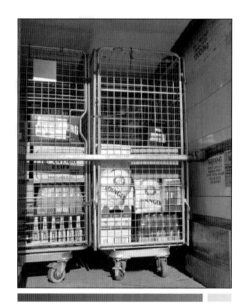

Empty or loaded skips may be carried either on dedicated skip lorries or on flatbed vehicles. It is recommended that skips are carried on skip lorries wherever possible, as it can be very difficult to adequately secure a skip on a flatbed vehicle.

Loaded or partly-loaded skips should not be stacked on top of each other for transport, even on a dedicated skip lorry. The lower skip does not provide a stable base. There is a risk of the upper skip/s moving under sudden braking, or falling from the side of the vehicle under a combined steering and braking manoeuvre (for example, swerving to avoid another road user). Some skip lorries have a shaft connecting the upper ends of the lifting arms and this is used by some operators to "press down" on stacked skips. This is not recommended, as the use of the lifting arms for load restraint could lead to crack growth, which can result in sudden failure even at low loads.

The lifting arms of skip lorries should be inspected every 12 months by a competent person in order to comply with LOLER.

LOLER stands for the Lifting Operations and Lifting Equipment Regulations 1998. They require that lifting equipment provided for use at work is:

- Strong and stable enough for use

- Positioned and installed to minimise risk

- Used safely

- Subject to ongoing thorough examination

Securing methods for different load types

8. Vehicles and plant equipment

Vehicles and plant equipment can be transported on specialised vehicles such as car transporters, on flatbed vehicles, or on lowloaders.

Passenger cars and light vans should ideally be transported on car transporters. At least two wheels of each car should be strapped down using wheel tethers, and chocks or blocking should be used on cars at the front and rear of the transporting vehicle to minimise the risk of load detachment.

Cars and light vans transported on flatbed or lowloader vehicles should be strapped down using wheel tethers on all four wheels, and chocked or blocked if necessary.

Heavy goods vehicles carried by 'piggyback' should be lashed to the transporting vehicle, preferably using chain lashings. Chocks should be used on each wheel if there is no other physical barrier to movement. Operators should be aware that the stability of the transporting vehicle can be significantly reduced when carrying vehicles by 'piggyback'. The transporting vehicle should be a lowloader body type, and it may be necessary to drive at a lower speed than usual and avoid roads with severe camber or particularly tight bends to reduce the risk of rollover or load detachment. Plant equipment is usually secured using chains in direct lashing. This is adequate as long as chains are used in opposed pairs: if a chain is pulling in one direction, another chain should be pulling in the opposite direction. It is very important to make sure that the load is prevented from moving in any direction.

Securing methods for different load types

9. Scrap metal

Scrap metal, including scrap cars, should be transported with caution as it is a high-density load and could cause a serious accident if it falls off the vehicle during the journey or while unloading.

Scrap metal also often features sharp edges that can easily cut through webbing lashings, so it may be better to use chain lashings. The friction between the load and the vehicle load bed is likely to be very low so it is important to use a good number of lashings. You should think carefully before stacking scrap vehicles, as a stack can be extremely unstable.

10. Containers and cabins

Containers and cabins (typically mobile work cabins being delivered to construction or manufacturing sites) should ideally be transported on vehicles where they can be secured by twist lock fastenings. However, they are often transported on flatbed vehicles and it is important to ensure that they are secured adequately as a load detachment could kill or seriously injure other road users.

The friction between a metal container or cabin and the load bed is likely to be low, so it is recommended that friction matting is used between the load and the load bed to increase the friction.

If possible, the load should be placed in contact with the vehicle headboard. Where this is not possible, or where there is an operational reason for loading back from the headboard, blocking or an intermediate headboard should be used to physically prevent the load from sliding forward. Lashings should then be used to secure the load to the vehicle bed.

Securing methods for different load types

11. Dangerous goods

12. Kegs and barrels

Any load shift can be dangerous, but if the load is hazardous the consequences of load shift can be disastrous. It is therefore very important to ensure that hazardous loads are well secured for road transport.

Dangerous goods are liquid or solid substances that have been tested and assessed against internationally-agreed criteria - a process called classification - and found to be potentially hazardous. Dangerous goods are assigned to different Classes depending on the most significant hazard.

If you are transporting dangerous goods, you should be aware of the requirements of the Carriage of Dangerous Goods and Use of Transportable Pressure Equipment Regulations 2009 and the European Agreement concerning the International Carriage of Dangerous Goods by Road 2009.

Kegs and barrels should be secured to prevent them moving while the vehicle is in motion and also to reduce the risk of them falling out of the vehicle during unloading. This is particularly important for kerbside deliveries to smaller premises where pedestrians are at risk of being hit by something falling from the vehicle. Lashing loads at multi-drop kerbside delivery sites may put the driver at more risk, and other restraint methods should be used if possible.

Small and/or breakable items should be transported in stillages if no other method can be used.

Securing methods for different load types

13. Scaffolding equipment

14. Building materials

Scaffolding equipment may comprise of poles, boards and ancillary equipment, and is often transported on flatbed vehicles.

As with any other load, scaffolding equipment should be loaded so that it doesn't slide or topple under normal driving conditions.

Fold-up sides and a rear gate can help to prevent load movement and allow equipment to be transported without lashings, as long as the load is not stacked higher than the sides.

The load should be placed in contact with the headboard if possible. If a gap is left, an intermediate bulkhead (which can be constructed from scaffold boards), blocking or dunnage can be used to prevent movement, or lashings can be used over the load.

Stack the load carefully and support it if necessary so that it won't become unstable once the vehicle is moving.

Stone, bricks, concrete and similar products can be particularly dangerous if they become detached from the vehicle. Even small stones, which may not cause much damage to a car, could kill or seriously injure a pedestrian or cyclist if they become detached at speed. Building materials should be secured to the vehicle, but containment should be considered in addition to restraint. Building products should be loaded from the headboard if possible. If lashings are used to secure the load, consider using edge protection or webbing sleeves to protect the lashings from wear.

Example loading docket (single site road delivery)

Consignor:...............................	Delivering to:......................................
Address:.................................	Address:..
....	....
Contact:.................................	Contact:...

Loaded on:....../....../.......... by...

| Description of load:... .... | Mass in tonnes:......................... |
| | Number of separate items:........... |

Trailer type: Curtain-sided ☐ Box-sided ☐ Flatbed ☐ Other ☐

Securing equipment: Webbing straps ☐ Chain ☐ Fixing bar ☐

Blocking ☐ Other ☐

Load checked by:............................. ....